*Set design and photo by Nathan Heverin*

A scene from the New York production of *Sin (A Cardinal Deposed)*.

# SIN
## (A CARDINAL DEPOSED)

### BY MICHAEL MURPHY

DRAMATISTS
PLAY SERVICE
INC.

# ACKNOWLEDGMENTS

The author would like to thank Mrs. Maryetta Dussourd, for allowing the use of her story, and the McSorley family, for allowing Patrick's. The author would also like to thank attorney Mitchell Garabedian for his invaluable assistance. The documents used to construct the play came from the websites of www.bishop-accountability.org and the Boston *Globe* (which won the Pulitzer Prize for its coverage of the events explored in this play).

# AUTHOR'S NOTE

SIN (A CARDINAL DEPOSED) was constructed from the depositions of Cardinal Bernard F. Law, Archbishop of Boston, in two civil suits involving priests of the archdiocese accused of child molestation. These were conducted in 2002 and 2003. Additional material came from internal church documents that entered the legal proceedings. The supervising court ordered these documents, along with the deposition transcripts, released to the public. The documents are housed at www.bishop-accountability.org (a non-profit organization that catalogues documents on the scandal worldwide) and the Boston *Globe's* site (the product of the *Globe's* Pulitzer Prize–winning coverage of the scandal as it played out in Boston), www.boston.com/globe/spotlight/abuse/. Cardinal Law's opening speech came from remarks he made at Holy Cross. Judge Sweeney's opening speech were edited from her remarks from the bench. Structurally, the play combines the two civil suits into one, since they covered a lot of the same ground. Also, the play distills the dozen attorneys who appear in the depositions into two composite characters, one for each side, and gives them fictious names — "Orson Krieger" for the plaintiffs and "William Varley" for Cardinal Law. All other names are as they appeared in the documents. Exhibit numbers were not available for all evidence referred to in the proceedings. For consistency, some exhibits were given reference numbers by the playwright. A portion of the royalties from productions of the play has been donated to survivors of clergy sexual abuse.

SIN (A CARDINAL DEPOSED) was produced by The New Group at the Clurman Theatre (Scott Elliot, Artistic Director; Geoffrey Rich, Executive Director; Ian Morgan, Associate Artistic Director) in New York City, opening on October 11, 2004. It was directed by Carl Forsman; the set design was by Nathan Heverin; the costume design was by Theresa Squire; the lighting design was by Josh Bradford; the sound design was by Sam Doerr; and the production stage manager was Valerie A. Peterson. The cast was as follows:

CARDINAL BERNARD F. LAW ............................ John Cullum
ANONYMOUS VICTIM, ANONYMOUS FATHER,
FR. CHABOT, DR. SWORDS, BISHOP D'ARCY,
FR. MCGEADY, FR. FLATLEY, PASTOR WESTON,
BISHOP BANKS, FR./BISHOP MCCORMACK,
DR. MULLINS, SPEAKER #1 ................................... Dan Daily
MARYETTA DUSSOURD, JUDGE SWEENY,
MARGARET GALLANT, SR. ANNE,
ANONYMOUS MOTHER, DOLORES STEVENS,
WILMA HIGGS, JACKIE GAUVREAU,
SPEAKER #2 ........................................................Cynthia Darlow
ORSON KRIEGER ............................................ Thomas Jay Ryan
PATRICK MCSORLEY ................................... Pablo T. Schreiber
WILLIAM VARLEY ............................. John Leonard Thompson

# CHARACTERS

Cardinal Bernard F. Law, Archbishop of Boston
Judge Constance Sweeney, Suffolk Superior Court
Orson Krieger, attorney for the plaintiffs
William Varley, attorney for Cardinal Law
Patrick McSorley, plaintiff

Anonymous Mother
Anonymous Father
Mrs. Margaret Gallant, a concerned family member
Mrs. Maryetta Dussourd, a concerned mother
Mrs. Dolores Stevens, a concerned parishioner
Mrs. Wilma T. Higgs, a concerned parishioner
Ms. Jackie Gauvreau, a concerned parishioner
Anonymous Employee, Massachusetts Department of Social
Services, a victim
Sister Anne, a concerned religious
Father Arthur Chabot, a concerned religious
Father McGeady, a concerned religious
Bishop D'Arcy, a concerned religious
Father Chabot, a concerned religious
Pastor Weston, a concerned religious
Father Flatley, archdiocese of Boston
Bishop Banks, archdiocese of Boston
Father McCormack, archdiocese of Boston
Dr. Mullins
Dr. Swords
Speaker #1
Speaker #2

# PLACE

Deposition room in Suffolk Superior Court, Boston, Massachusetts.

# TIME

May 8, 2002.

# SIN
## (A CARDINAL DEPOSED)

*At rise, spotlight on Cardinal Law.*

CARDINAL.  Some have suggested that — in the light of the events of the past weeks and months surrounding a public airing of the way the Church in this archdiocese, and I in particular, have handled the cases of sexual abuse by priests — that I should resign as archbishop. I respect the opinion of those who have reached that conclusion, but I must tell you — before God — that is not the conclusion that I reach in prayer. I do not intend to resign, not as an act of stubbornness. We have acknowledged, that in retrospect, and that is a very important word, in retrospect, that we made — I made — mistakes. But it's important to remember, I think, that a bishop is not a corporate executive; he's not a politician. He is a pastor; he is a teacher; he is a father. The ring I wear is a reminder that my relationship to the Church is like a marriage. And when there are problems in the family, you don't walk away. I have the ability to do something as your archbishop to make things better for the future. And I think that it would not serve the cause of protecting children if I were, at this point, to submit my resignation to the Holy Father. Thank you for listening. *(Spotlight on Judge Sweeney. Lights up on deposition room in Suffolk Superior Court, Boston. Krieger, McSorley, Cardinal, Varley enter.)*

JUDGE.  This court has significant concerns about Cardinal Law's availability for deposition in the matter of Patrick McSorley, Gregory Ford and eighty-six other plaintiffs versus Cardinal Bernard F. Law. The Cardinal's choice is not entirely belonging to him. If the pope tells him to go to Rome, he goes. This court finds no reason to delay this any longer. The deposition will commence Wednesday, May 8, 2002, starting at nine A.M. in Suffolk Superior Court, Boston, Massachusetts. It will be videotaped to stand as testimony if the

Cardinal is not available should this suit proceed to trial.

VARLEY. My name is William Varley. I appear for His Eminence Cardinal Law.

KRIEGER. Orson Krieger for the plaintiffs. With me today is a victim, and plaintiff, Patrick McSorley. This action has been brought against the defendant, Cardinal Bernard Law, for failing to protect the plaintiffs from sexual abuse by Roman Catholic priests of the Archdiocese of Boston. Those priests are not parties to this action. Rather, the plaintiffs have brought negligence claims against the defendant, Cardinal Law, who was their supervisor.

VARLEY. We would interpose a First Amendment objection as to any questions going to the internal workings of the church. I think it would be a more orderly deposition if we go forward with an agreement on the record that this objection applies to all testimony and motions to strike are reserved until time of trial.

KRIEGER. Agreed. I believe the court reporter has already administered the oath with the defendant?

VARLEY. He has. We can proceed.

KRIEGER. Good morning, Your Eminence.

CARDINAL. Good morning.

KRIEGER. I'd like to thank you, Cardinal Law, for coming in here today. One ground rule, very simple. If at any point you want to go over your testimony, modify or change your answers in any way, just indicate that to me and I'll let you do that. Do you understand?

CARDINAL. I do.

KRIEGER. If I refer to you as Cardinal, is that acceptable, Your Eminence?

CARDINAL. Sure.

KRIEGER. Would you state your name for the record?

CARDINAL. Yes. My name is Bernard Francis Law.

KRIEGER. Could you spell that, please?

CARDINAL. Bernard. Capital B-e-r-n-a-r-d. Francis. Capital F-r-a-n-c-i-s. Law. Capital L-a-w.

KRIEGER. Where do you reside?

CARDINAL. Brighton, Massachusetts, 2101 Commonwealth Avenue.

KRIEGER. And is that the Archbishop's residence?

CARDINAL. And office, that's right. I live over the store.

KRIEGER. Are you a citizen of the United States?

CARDINAL. I am.

KRIEGER. Are you a citizen of the Vatican State?

CARDINAL. I am.

KRIEGER. Are you a citizen of any other country that you know of?

CARDINAL. I was born in Mexico. I believe I could have dual citizenship, but I, in fact, do not.

KRIEGER. Where did you graduate high school?

CARDINAL. Charlotte Amalie in St. Thomas, Virgin Island.

KRIEGER. Could you spell that, please?

CARDINAL. Charlotte. Capital C-h-a-r-l-o-t-t-e. Amalie. Capital A-m-a-l-i-e.

KRIEGER. And where did you go to college?

CARDINAL. I went to Harvard. Capital H-a-r-v-a-r-d.

KRIEGER. Did you graduate with honors?

CARDINAL. No.

KRIEGER. What did you do next?

CARDINAL. I entered seminary.

KRIEGER. As a seminarian, did you ever assist in any parishes?

CARDINAL. Yes. During my six years in seminary, over the summers, I went on sick calls, taught religious education, tutored. I assisted in any way I could.

KRIEGER. After you were ordained a priest, what parish were you assigned to?

CARDINAL. St. Paul's in Vicksburg, Mississippi.

KRIEGER. At that time, Cardinal Law, did you believe or know that the sexual molestation of minors was a crime?

CARDINAL. You know, I have to say that in my early priesthood, the sexual molestation of minors wasn't even on my radar screen. It wasn't the issue that it is today.

KRIEGER. I'm sorry. The question was — when you were serving in Mississippi, did you know that individuals who molested children were committing crimes?

CARDINAL. Well, I thought I'd answered that question. Sexual molestation wasn't something that was before me. It didn't come up.

KRIEGER. So is it your testimony that you didn't know it was a crime?

CARDINAL. Well, certainly, if someone were to ask me, my presumption is, yes, of course, it's a crime.

KRIEGER. I don't mean to press you on this, but I don't think you've answered the specific question. Was the sexual molestation of children in the 1960s something that you knew to be a crime?

VARLEY. Objection. He's clearly answered it.

KRIEGER. All right. Were there any allegations of sexual misconduct by clergy that came to your attention while in Mississippi?

CARDINAL. No, although I believe there was a case I became aware of after I left Mississippi. But I have no active memory of that case prior to my departure.

KRIEGER. You just used the term "active memory" — "I have no active memory." I think I understand what you're saying, but I just want to make sure that I do —

CARDINAL. I don't remember.

KRIEGER. You don't remember. Are you familiar with the doctrine of broad and strict mental reservation?

CARDINAL. Yeah.

KRIEGER. Can you describe what that doctrine is, please?

CARDINAL. I'm not sure that I can describe it accurately. It feels like I'm in a moral theology exam here.

KRIEGER. Well, I don't want —

CARDINAL. If you could put the question another way and let me respond.

KRIEGER. Fine. Do either of those doctrines, moral or strict mental reservation, justify not telling the truth in certain situations?

CARDINAL. May I respond, Mr. Krieger, in this way, and I hope that it gets to what your question is asking: I am making neither broad nor narrow mental reservations in my response to your questions.

KRIEGER. I understand that.

CARDINAL. I am trying to respond to your questions as completely and honestly as I possibly can.

KRIEGER. Okay.

CARDINAL. And I have no reason to make mental reservations.

KRIEGER. But do you agree with me that the doctrine of broad mental reservation does, under some circumstances, permit someone who is a priest or a bishop of the Roman Catholic Church to make statements that are not technically true?

CARDINAL. I say to you as I sit before you under oath that I am making no mental reservations about withholding what I know to be the truth when you ask me a forthright question.

KRIEGER. Thank you.

CARDINAL. Certainly.

KRIEGER. Cardinal, how long did you serve in Mississippi?

CARDINAL. Until December of '73, when I became a bishop.

KRIEGER. Were you assigned to a new diocese?

CARDINAL. Springfield Cape–Giradeau in Missouri.

KRIEGER. Springfield–Cape Giradeau? Have I pronounced that correctly?

CARDINAL. Well, it's good enough.

KRIEGER. While you were the Bishop there, did you have reports that came to you about — I'm not asking for any names — reports of priests having inappropriate contact with children?

CARDINAL. Yes.

KRIEGER. Was there more than one instance while you were there?

CARDINAL. I don't recall more than one.

KRIEGER. So it wasn't an ordinary thing that you came across there?

CARDINAL. That's correct.

KRIEGER. Is the priest you received a report on still a priest?

CARDINAL. No.

KRIEGER. Sometime in 1984, were you named the Archbishop of Boston?

CARDINAL. January of '84 is when I found out.

KRIEGER. Why don't you, if you could, briefly describe what is an archdiocese.

CARDINAL. An archdiocese would be, if you will, a major diocese historically. The first diocese of Boston comprised all of New England. Very, very few priests and very, very few Catholics, a vast territory. Now the archdiocese of Boston constitutes about two million Catholics in the state of Massachusetts and a diocese each in Vermont, New Hampshire and Maine.

KRIEGER. In 1985, you became a cardinal; is that correct?

CARDINAL. Yes.

KRIEGER. And you're one of seventeen cardinals in the U.S.?

CARDINAL. There are twelve.

KRIEGER. You were elevated to cardinal by Pope John Paul II; is that correct?

CARDINAL. Correct.

KRIEGER. Cardinal Law, please turn to Exhibit 14, a letter dated October 1, 1964. *(Spotlight on Anonymous Mother.)*

ANONYMOUS MOTHER. We are taking the liberty of reporting directly to you the following serious events which took place a few weeks ago at St. Ann's parish in Marshfield. We trust that you in your wisdom will know how best to handle the matter. Our son, age twelve, is an altar boy at St. Ann's. While in the sacristy, Father Eugene O'Sullivan reached under our son's bathing trunks and touched him repeatedly in the private area. Our son says this has happened on previous occasions. The next day, we visited the rectory and reported the incident to the pastor, Father Finn, who said he would report this to the proper authorities and we could expect to be contacted. After waiting six weeks, we telephoned Father Finn and were shocked to hear him say he had not reported the matter because he had received no further complaints. When we asked if he attempted to question any of the other altar boys, or even Father O'Sullivan, he replied, "Oh, no, I couldn't do that." *(Back to deposition.)*

KRIEGER. Have you ever seen this document before?

VARLEY. Do you mean before today?

CARDINAL. I have not.

KRIEGER. This was in your files, Cardinal Law.

CARDINAL. Excuse me — the Archdiocese's files.

KRIEGER. So it's your testimony that you've never seen this document?

VARLEY. Again, Orson, before today?

KRIEGER. Mr. Varley, if the Cardinal doesn't understand the question, he is free to indicate that and I will rephrase the question so he understands it. But suggesting the question is one he can't understand is not consistent with the rules set forth by the judge. I suggest you look at the rules on conduct during depositions.

VARLEY. I appreciate the observation, Mr. Krieger, but if I am going to take advice in how to conduct depositions, you wouldn't be on the list of those I'd come to.

KRIEGER. This is a very important case, Mr. Varley, with very serious allegations. I'm trying to get answers from your client.

VARLEY. I understand this is an important case. It's important for the plaintiffs, for the defendants, for everybody who has a concern about child abuse. It's important for everybody, Mr. Krieger. I understand that every bit as well as you do.

KRIEGER. Are you done?

VARLEY. Next question.

KRIEGER. Do you remember the question, Cardinal Law?

CARDINAL. I think I do, but I'd appreciate your refreshing my memory.

KRIEGER. I'd be happy to do that. Believe me, it is not my intent here to embarrass or annoy you in any way —

CARDINAL. Well, you're certainly not embarrassing me, Mr. Krieger.

KRIEGER. Shall we continue then?

CARDINAL. But I must tell you that I am attempting to answer your questions as fully as I can.

KRIEGER. I appreciate that.

CARDINAL. Fine.

KRIEGER. Now. We just reviewed a letter concerning a Father Eugene O'Sullivan. From a mother who alleged that Father O'Sullivan molested her son. Have you seen this document before?

CARDINAL. Mr. Krieger, that letter is dated 1964. It is addressed to Cardinal Cushing, my predecessor's predecessor. Cardinal Cushing died in 1970. His successor, Cardinal Medeiros, died in 1983. I succeeded Cardinal Medeiros.

KRIEGER. Alright.

CARDINAL. When I arrived in Boston in 1984, I assumed that priests in place had been appointed appropriately. It did not enter into my mind to second-guess my predecessors, and it simply was not in the culture of the day to function otherwise.

KRIEGER. Now I'd like for us to talk about a Father Joseph Birmingham. Do you know who he is?

CARDINAL. Yes.

KRIEGER. We have some documents. They're allegations going back to 1964 on Father Birmingham. Um, but we're going to, we're going to talk about your tenure, what you did in a case involving a priest with allegations of sexual abuse.

VARLEY. I object to that kind of preamble from counsel. Ask a question.

KRIEGER. Let's turn to Exhibit 47, a letter to you from a concerned father. *(Spotlight on Anonymous Father.)*

ANONYMOUS FATHER. Dear Cardinal Law. I am writing to you about Father Joe Birmingham, who I've recently read was taken out of St. James' Parish in Salem in the early 1970s after allegations of sexual abuse of several altar boys. I want to know if he is the same Joe Birmingham who is the current pastor in my parish at St. Ann's. I am concerned about whether my son, an altar boy there, has been abused by Father Birmingham. I am also concerned because I have heard that Father Birmingham might have AIDS. *(Back to deposition.)*

KRIEGER. This letter is from a father concerned about this priest possibly having molested his son, is that right?

CARDINAL. Well, he's not making a charge that he's been molested, but that he could be in danger.

KRIEGER. You would regard this as a very important communication; is that correct?

CARDINAL. Sure, it's an important letter.

KRIEGER. Now let's turn to 22, a letter dated April 14, 1987, from Bishop McCormack — then Father McCormack, your secretary for Ministerial Personnel. He wrote back to this man. *(Spot on Bishop McCormack.)*

BISHOP MCCORMACK. His Eminence, Cardinal Law, received your letter and asked me to look into the matter for him. I contacted Father Birmingham and asked him specifically about the matter you expressed and he assured me there is absolutely no factual basis to your concern. Therefore, I see no need for you to raise this question with your son. I hope this allays any concern you may have. Sincerely yours in Christ ... *(Back to deposition.)*

KRIEGER. Have you seen this letter before?

CARDINAL. I have no memory of having seen it.

KRIEGER. Do you recall, as the letter states, instructing Father McCormack to look into the man's charges?

CARDINAL. No — and I don't see how I could have. If you look at the letter, you'll note there are two stamps. The first stamp on the right says *Not Acknowledged at Residence*. The second stamp to the left says *Received, Office of Ministerial Personnel*. Which means the letter was opened by my personal secretary, but instead of him sending it on to me, he referred it to Father McCormack in Ministerial Personnel for follow-up.

KRIEGER. Why would a letter setting forth serious allegations of sexual misconduct by a priest be stamped *Not Acknowledged at Residence*? What would be the purpose of such a policy?

CARDINAL. To ensure that the letter was handled in an appropriate way by the appropriate person. If you don't think that was a right way to do it, you're entitled to your opinion, but I think that it's a rather good way to handle the volume of business that comes across my desk.

KRIEGER. Father McCormack's response to this man says: "His Eminence, Cardinal Law, received your letter and asked me to look into the matter for him." If you're this man, wouldn't the only interpretation be that you had actually spoken with Father McCormack and asked him to look into it?

CARDINAL. I cannot tell you what somebody else would have thought or not thought.

KRIEGER. Is this an attempt, Cardinal Law, this *Not Acknowledged at Residence* stamp, to distance yourself from these allegations of sexual abuse?

VARLEY. I object to the insulting tone of that question.

CARDINAL. Quite the contrary, Mr. Krieger. That was an attempt to be sure that things were handled in an orderly, systematic, timely fashion. And I rely on my staff to help me in a wide range of questions that come across my desk. Educational matters, financial. This particular concern was handled by the secretary for Ministerial Personnel, Father McCormack. I don't see that it was anything other than a desire to be sure that these and all matters were handled well.

KRIEGER. Cardinal, do you remember when you first heard of Father John Geoghan? *(Pronounced "Gay-gun.")*

CARDINAL. I do not.

KRIEGER. I'd like us to look at 226, a letter from a Mrs. Margaret Gallant. This letter is addressed to you, Cardinal Law. *(Spotlight on Margaret Gallant.)*

MARGARET GALLANT. Dear Excellency. It is with deep regret that I impart the following. There is a priest at St. Brendan's, a Father John Geoghan, who has been known to molest boys. He was sent for treatments and after returning to parish duties maintained a low profile for quite a while. Lately, however, he has been seen in the company of many boys, to the extent of dropping them off at their homes as late as 9:30 P.M. Our family is very deeply rooted in the Church with a firm love of holy orders. We do not accuse this priest of sin, since we are all sinners, but rather we speak here of crime. Since three of my nephews and my four grand-nephews had dealings with the priest, I am certain of these facts. My heart is broken over the whole situation and it is a burden to my conscience that the parish is left in the dark while I know the danger its children are in. My heart also breaks that my first offering to you is this cup of bitter wine with no taste of joy. And so, it is to you, my dearly loved Archbishop, that I pass this burden with hope and trust. *(Back to deposition.)*

KRIEGER. Have you seen this letter, Cardinal?

CARDINAL. I do not recall having received it.

VARLEY. Your Eminence, the question is actually whether you've seen it.

CARDINAL. Oh, yes. I've seen it before. In the past few weeks, I've had the opportunity to review many documents. But I can tell you that I don't recall receiving this letter at the time.

KRIEGER. On the envelope, there's some handwriting. Do you know whose handwriting that is?

CARDINAL. That would be my handwriting.

KRIEGER. And what does your handwriting say?

CARDINAL. It's addressed to Bishop Daily and says "urgent, please follow through."

KRIEGER. And Bishop Daily had what position in the Archdiocese?

CARDINAL. Bishop Daily was in effect chief operating officer, the person upon whom I would rely to assist me in the administration of the archdiocese.

KRIEGER. In your first year as archbishop, you didn't get a large number of letters informing you that a priest in the archdiocese had been molesting boys; is that correct?

CARDINAL. That's correct.

KRIEGER. So a letter like this would have been more of the exception?

CARDINAL. It would have been.

KRIEGER. In 1984, was it the practice for someone else, say your secretary, to ask you to handwrite a note to Bishop Daily without having you read what it was concerning?

CARDINAL. Are you referencing the envelope here? I must say — no. No one would tell me to put that note on. That kind of a note is a note that I would put on — having absorbed the content of whatever the backup, whatever the backup letter is. So the only thing I can say ... That is my signature, I wrote that. I would be lying to you if I said I recall having seen this letter before, but I can't sit here before you and say that I saw it when I don't think I did, when I don't remember seeing it.

KRIEGER. Would it be fair to say that when you wrote notes to Bishop Daily, you didn't usually write "urgent"?

CARDINAL. That means what it means, you know — that I considered this an urgent matter, and that I wanted it followed through on, and I expected Bishop Daily to follow through for me — to do whatever it takes to deal with this thing expeditiously and correctly.

KRIEGER. Did you have a conversation with Bishop Daily about Mrs. Gallant?

CARDINAL. I don't recall having a conversation with Bishop Daily on this matter.

KRIEGER. But the record seems to indicate that you took Margaret Gallant's letter seriously at the time and asked Bishop Daily to address it in a serious manner?

CARDINAL. That's correct.

KRIEGER. And address it quickly.

CARDINAL. That's correct.

KRIEGER. Do you remember having a conversation with Bishop Daily about terminating Father Geoghan at St. Brendan's following this allegation?

CARDINAL. I do not recall a conversation with him on that.

KRIEGER. But you did remove Father Geoghan from St. Brendan's at this time; is that correct?

CARDINAL. That's correct.

KRIEGER. And you removed him over allegations of sexual misconduct involving minors; is that correct?

CARDINAL. I knew that there had been a problem at St. Brendan's, but I had only been Archbishop of Boston a short time when this issue came to my attention. I didn't know the details, the history.

KRIEGER. At this time, Boston would have been the third or fourth largest Catholic diocese in the country; is that correct?

CARDINAL. Yes.

KRIEGER. With over 400 parishes and approximately 215 schools; correct?

CARDINAL. That's correct.

KRIEGER. And there were tens of thousands of children being served at CCD classes in those parishes and schools; correct?

CARDINAL. Yes.

KRIEGER. Given all this, what written policies were in place to minimize or mitigate the possibility that children would be sexually abused by priests of the Archdiocese?

CARDINAL. There was no written policy until 1993 — a policy, as you know, that I put in place. As I recall, even you had some positive things to say about what we did in 1993.

KRIEGER. There were many things said in 1993.

CARDINAL. Well, I appreciated what you had to say very, very much.

KRIEGER. So with no written policy from this period for us to look at, Cardinal Law, what was the practice in dealing with allegations of child sexual abuse by priests?

CARDINAL. I viewed this as a pathology, an illness, so consequently, I, not being a psychiatrist, my modus operandi was to rely upon those whom I considered to have an expertise that I lacked in assessing what it is that this person could safely do or not do. I relied on those assisting me in administration of the Archdiocese to

17

handle this process. I relied on those persons to consult with, to refer to either physicians, psychiatrists or medical institutions that seemed worthy. I didn't enter into the decision as to this physician, that treatment center. I really relied on those persons who would be more knowledgeable because they would be following up.

KRIEGER. So the procedure was to send the priest to a doctor?

CARDINAL. That's correct.

KRIEGER. You just wanted to have someone say you could send him back to parish duty — you didn't really qualify it more than that, correct?

VARLEY. Objection.

CARDINAL. I expected a professionally competent person to make the recommendation.

KRIEGER. Had you explained the criteria to Bishop Banks or Bishop Daily what you meant by "professionally competent"?

CARDINAL. I don't recall doing that. It seemed to me that it was obvious.

KRIEGER. Do you think that it is obvious, looking back now?

VARLEY. Objection.

KRIEGER. Was this allegation against Father Geoghan reported to the authorities?

CARDINAL. As you know, we currently report every credible case of abuse to public authorities.

KRIEGER. I'm not talking about today, Cardinal Law. I'm asking what you did in 1984.

CARDINAL. It was our conviction that it was more appropriate for the victim or parent of the victim to make that decision. We felt that we would inhibit some victims from coming forward if we immediately reported to the authorities. I see now that that should have been done.

KRIEGER. Cardinal Law, please turn to 35, a letter you wrote to Father John Geoghan. Do you see that?

CARDINAL. Yes.

KRIEGER. It's dated October 31, 1984, roughly five weeks after you removed him from St. Brendan's. Do you see that?

CARDINAL. Yes.

KRIEGER. In this letter, you inform Father Geoghan that you are returning him to parish duty at St. Julia's. Do you see that?

CARDINAL. I do.

KRIEGER. And then you go on to say to Father Geoghan: "I am confident that you will render fine priestly service to the people of

God in St. Julia Parish." Do you see that?

VARLEY. I'm going to object to just reading something and asking the Cardinal whether he sees it and not asking any questions about it.

KRIEGER. Your objection is noted.

VARLEY. Well, that was the point of my making it.

KRIEGER. Okay.

VARLEY. We're wasting time, showing the Cardinal a document and asking him if he sees it.

KRIEGER. Alright. Let's just move on.

VARLEY. Thank you.

KRIEGER. Cardinal Law, are you aware of any documents from any doctor or psychiatrist between Margaret Gallant's letter and the day you assigned Father Geoghan to St. Julia's — a document indicating it was safe to send Father Geoghan back to parish assignment?

CARDINAL. What I am aware of is my expectation — and that expectation was understood by those who assisted me — that no one could be put back into parish assignment unless there were a medical attestation that it was safe to do so. Now, I do not have recall about documents that are in the files going back eighteen years. But I can say, without a shadow of doubt, that Father Geoghan would not have received a new appointment unless we had received the proper attestation.

KRIEGER. Turn to exhibit 229, a handwritten letter from a Robert Mullins, M.D., a family physician. *(Spotlight on Dr. Mullins.)*

DR MULLINS. Father John Geoghan, a longtime friend and patient of mine, has recently terminated his ministry at St. Brendan's Parish due to' a rather unfortunate traumatic experience. Following a brief, but beneficial, respite from his duties, Father Geoghan has adjusted remarkably well. In my opinion, he is now able to resume full Pastoral activities without any need for specific restrictions. *(Back to deposition.)*

KRIEGER. Your Eminence, Dr. Mullins recommends that Geoghan "be allowed to return to full pastoral activities" —

CARDINAL. Without any need for specific restrictions.

KRIEGER. Now, unless I'm mistaken, this is it. This was the medical certification that says Father Geoghan was fine to return to parish ministry.

VARLEY. Is that a question?

KRIEGER. Did you ever have a conversation with Father Geoghan's superior at St. Julia's about why you removed him from St. Brendan's?

CARDINAL. I don't recall personally having had such a conversation.

KRIEGER. Would you have wanted Father Geoghan's superior at St. Julia's to be aware of the allegations that led you to remove him from his previous assignment?

CARDINAL. Yes, I would have wanted that.

KRIEGER. And how would you have seen that that information would have been conveyed to him?

CARDINAL. My presumption would be that those assisting me in handling these matters would have done what was appropriate.

KRIEGER. Were the parishioners at St. Julia's made aware of the issues with Father Geoghan?

CARDINAL. As you know, we did not, as a matter of policy, go to parishes where an allegation of sexual abuse of a child against the priest had been made. These cases tended to be handled with a desire on the part of the victim for confidentiality. That was the culture for handling those cases. I have said — that culture was wrong. It's essential to go back to the parish. In our efforts now, we do that. But that's now. I wish to God it were possible to go back in time, but it isn't.

KRIEGER. Could you answer my question now?

VARLEY. Objection.

KRIEGER. Were the parishioners at St. Julia's informed when Father Geoghan arrived that he had been removed from his previous assignment because of allegations of sexual abuse of a minor?

CARDINAL. Mr. Krieger, the answer to that is no, based on my prior response, which I have already given you, that our present policy is to inform parishes. It was not the policy in '84, '85, '86, '87, '88, '89, '90, '91, '92, '93, '94, '95, '96, '97, '98, '99, 2000 or 2001 to go back to parishes. I see now that that should have been done, but we did not do that. So it was not done in '84. Was this adequate in retrospect? No, it was not adequate in retrospect. Our present policy is to inform the parishes. But, unfortunately, you can't undo the past.

KRIEGER. Please turn to Exhibit 166, a letter by Bishop John D'Arcy, dated roughly a month into Father Geoghan's assignment at St. Julia's. *(Spotlight on Bishop D'Arcy.)*

BISHOP D'ARCY. Just a word on the assignment of Father John Geoghan at St. Julia's. Father Geoghan has a history of homosexual involvement with young boys. I understand his recent abrupt departure from St. Brendan's may be related to this problem. St. Julia's has been a troubled parish. If something happens, the parishioners, already angry, will be convinced that the archdiocese has no concern for their welfare. While no parish can handle these shocking situations that we have witnessed recently, this parish is most vulnerable. I wonder if Father Geoghan should not be reduced to just weekend work while receiving some kind of therapy. *(Back to deposition.)*

KRIEGER. Do you recall seeing this letter?

CARDINAL. I don't have a recall of this letter, no.

KRIEGER. In 1985, was Bishop D'Arcy given a new assignment?

CARDINAL. Do you mean outside the diocese?

KRIEGER. Outside the diocese.

CARDINAL. Fort Wayne.

KRIEGER. Indiana?

CARDINAL. It's a good diocese. Notre Dame is there, of course.

KRIEGER. You had the power, after receiving this letter from Bishop D'Arcy, to remove John Geoghan from St. Julia's; correct?

CARDINAL. I had the power to do that.

KRIEGER. You do know that after Bishop D'Arcy's letter was received, Father Geoghan continued as a full-time parish priest; no change was made with respect to his work at St. Julia's?

CARDINAL. That's correct.

KRIEGER. Cardinal Law, from your knowledge of human behavior, would you agree with me that one of the things that you look for in determining future behavior is what has happened in the past?

CARDINAL. I would agree with that as a general statement with the understanding that two things can impact future behavior.

KRIEGER. Right.

CARDINAL. One is a medical intervention in terms both of therapy and drugs, if it's a psychological problem. And then another thing that can impact is, while it's much, much — it's impossible to predict —

KRIEGER. Right.

CARDINAL. — but which does impact — and I truly believe does change human behavior — is the grace of God.

KRIEGER. Cardinal, you would agree with me, at least with respect to John Geoghan at St. Julia's, neither treatment nor the grace of God changed his behavior.

VARLEY. Objection.

KRIEGER. Well, over the next five years, John Geoghan was accused of molesting children at St. Julia's; is that correct?

CARDINAL. Yes.

KRIEGER. And you removed him from St. Julia's and sent him for assessment at the Institute of Living; is that not correct?

CARDINAL. Assessment and a treatment, yes.

KRIEGER. Let's turn to 104, the written discharge report dated December, 1989, from Dr. Robert Swords after Father Geoghan spent three months at the Institute. *(Spot on Dr. Swords.)*

DR. SWORDS. Let me first say that we judge Father Geoghan to be clinically quite safe to resume his pastoral ministry after observation, evaluation and treatment here for three months. The probability that he would sexually act out again is quite low. However, we cannot guarantee that it could not reoccur. It is both reasonable and therapeutic for him to be reassigned back to his parish. *(Back to deposition.)*

KRIEGER. Were there any restrictions placed on Father Geoghan in terms of access to minors?

CARDINAL. The critical sentence is the final sentence where the report states: "It is both reasonable and therapeutic for him to be reassigned back to his parish."

KRIEGER. Did they mean therapeutic for John Geoghan or therapeutic for the children of St. Julia's?

VARLEY. Objection, argumentative.

KRIEGER. After receiving this report, Cardinal, you sent Father Geoghan back to St. Julia's; is that correct?

CARDINAL. Yes.

KRIEGER. Without any restrictions on his access to children; correct?

CARDINAL. Correct. But —

KRIEGER. When the Institute of Living stated it could not guarantee that John Geoghan's acting out with children would not reoccur, why would you return him to parish duty without some restriction on his access to children?

CARDINAL. The discharge diagnosis of "atypical pedophilia in remission" refers to a condition in the past, the symptoms no longer in evidence or under firm control.

KRIEGER. We can both read selective sentences of this report. The Institute of Living did state that it could not guarantee that his problem of sexual molestation would not reoccur; correct?

CARDINAL. Yes.

KRIEGER. Would you say the protection of children in programs sponsored by the Archdiocese has been a top priority for you since you arrived in Boston?

CARDINAL. Yes.

KRIEGER. So when you returned Father Geoghan to St. Julia's, why were there no restrictions placed on him in terms of his access to children?

VARLEY. Do you believe you have answered that question?

CARDINAL. I believe I've answered it a hundred different ways.

VARLEY. Then I'm going to instruct him not to answer. This is becoming abusive.

KRIEGER. Do you recall giving any consideration to putting John Geoghan where he would not regularly have contact with children?

CARDINAL. Mr. Krieger, you may view this as selectively reading from this report, but all I can say to you is that the operative word from the Institute of Living impacting my decision to return Father Geoghan to St. Julia's is, "It is both reasonable and therapeutic for him to be reassigned back to his parish." Whether or not you think that was wise, whether or not I think it is wise, at this point, is irrelevant. It was on the basis of that recommendation that I had to make the decision and the Institute of Living carried a considerable weight in the decision.

KRIEGER. Did you also place considerable weight on this sentence: "We cannot guarantee that it could not reoccur"?

CARDINAL. Mr. Krieger, I don't want to appear exasperated, but I am. Because, you know, there's a reasonableness on my part, but for me to make an assignment of this kind — I am not a psychiatrist, I am not a psychologist — I need — the issue here for me was whether or not someone who had manifested this kind of pathological behavior could reasonably be reassigned in terms of risk involved. And so you send somebody away to find that out. I can't make that judgment. I was relying on the Institute of Living to indicate what is appropriate in the assignment of this priest.

KRIEGER. But the decision was made to assign John Geoghan to work in a parish without any restrictions on his access to children; is that not correct?

CARDINAL. He would have been involved with children, teaching.

KRIEGER. Please turn to exhibit 31, a letter from you to Father Geoghan, dated December 30, 1994. Do you see that?

CARDINAL. I do.

KRIEGER. Would you please read it?

CARDINAL. "Dear Father Geoghan. I was sorry to learn of the

23

recent allegations made about you at St. Julia's. I realize — "

KRIEGER. So the Institute of Living was right to have warned you that they could not guarantee Father Geoghan would not act out again. The sexual abuse hadn't stopped, had it?

VARLEY. Objection — argumentative.

KRIEGER. Cardinal Law ... Would you please finish reading the letter?

CARDINAL. "I realize this is a difficult time for you and for those close to you. If I — "

KRIEGER. Did you also believe when you wrote this letter that it was a difficult time for the victims of Father Geoghan?

VARLEY. Objection. Argumentative and obviously —

CARDINAL. You know, Mr. Krieger, I just wonder if you want to rethink that question —

KRIEGER. No, I really don't, Cardinal.

CARDINAL. — because, obviously, I did. But I'm writing to Father Geoghan.

KRIEGER. Could you answer the question, please?

CARDINAL. The answer is — of course.

KRIEGER. Could you please finish reading the letter, Cardinal?

CARDINAL. "If I can be of help to you in some way, please contact me. Be assured you are remembered in my prayers. With warm personal regards, I am, sincerely yours in Christ."

KRIEGER. So you were offering to be of assistance to John Geoghan; correct? *(Patrick McSorley suddenly exits. Krieger starts to go after him, but the Cardinal checks him, drawing him back with his answer.)*

CARDINAL. John Geoghan was a priest of this Archdiocese. If you'll note from the address, he is not at St. Julia's at this point. He's been assigned to an office where he does not have contact with children. He was effectively retired. And, yes, there is an offer to be of some help in what had to be a very difficult moment for him.

KRIEGER. I understand that, Cardinal Law, and my question is, did you send out any letters offering to be of help to any of the victims of Father Geoghan who had come forward?

VARLEY. I object to that question as being insulting. It's obviously grandstanding. It serves no legitimate purposes of deposition, and it's harassing, clearly harassing.

KRIEGER. Can you answer the question, please, Cardinal?

CARDINAL. Yes. And I would agree with my counsel that this is a harassing question.

KRIEGER. You may think it's not a question that you wish to answer but —
CARDINAL. No, no.
VARLEY. Why don't you go on to something that's relevant?
KRIEGER. This is very relevant.
VARLEY. Not to this case. How does it lead to —
KRIEGER. If you're instructing him not to answer the question, then so instruct him and we will continue the deposition. I have no problem with that. But I'm pressing the question.
VARLEY. The rules of this deposition talk about coming to the assistance of a witness when the questions are harassing, insulting and serve no useful purpose. I'm not just going to sit here like a potted plant.
KRIEGER. It's insulting for me to ask whether or not he wrote to any victim of sexual abuse? I really don't see how that's an insulting question.
VARLEY. It's a grandstanding question. It's not for any legitimate purpose, but rather to adulate your ego and appeal to your clients and the press.
KRIEGER. Well, Mr. Varley —
VARLEY. But answer, Cardinal, if you like.
CARDINAL. I would like to answer it, if I may.
KRIEGER. You would?
CARDINAL. Yes. My interaction with victims was carried out through my Delegate in whom I had full confidence — and still do. I do not recall sending any letters myself.
KRIEGER. I would like us to look at exhibit seventy-two, a memo you wrote to Father Geoghan, dated October, 1996. Do you have that?
CARDINAL. I do.
KRIEGER. Would you please read it aloud?
CARDINAL. "Dear Father Geoghan. I am granting your request for retirement status. As you know, it is unusual for a man of your age to be granted this status. However, your particular situation makes it advisable. Yours has been an effective life of ministry, sadly impaired by illness. On behalf of those you have served well, and in my own name, I would like to thank you. I understand yours is a painful situation. The Passion we share can indeed seem unbearable and unrelenting. We are our best selves when we respond in honesty and trust. God bless you, Jack. Asking god's blessing on you and those you love ... "

KRIEGER. "Yours has been an effective life of ministry ... "
When you wrote that, Cardinal, you knew there had been a string
of allegations of sexual misconduct against John Geoghan since
you arrived in Boston?

CARDINAL. That's why Father Geoghan was removed from
active ministry.

KRIEGER. But you considered his service to be an effective life of
ministry?

CARDINAL. This is an effort to be pastorally present to a priest
who, in his life, did minister well to a number of people, and at the
same time, terribly abused children. It's a mixture of light and of
darkness. And when you respond to an individual in the midst of
that kind of a situation, you, I think, appropriately, as a bishop, try
to remind that person that there has been some — there's been
good here; that your life is not defined simply by your evil deeds,
but your good deeds are also there. And yet, it's a call for him to
respond with honesty to his situation and trust. We sent him to
this place, Southdown, where we had hoped he would be helped.

KRIEGER. Since you knew that John Geoghan had committed
evil deeds, Cardinal, did you in any way undertake to locate other
victims of Father Geoghan who might need pastoral assistance?

CARDINAL. Again, I relied on my Delegate to assist me in ministry to victims.

KRIEGER. I need to take break at this point. *(Krieger exits to
search for McSorley. Spotlight on Maryetta Dussourd.)*

MARYETTA DUSSOURD. Um, Father Geoghan invited himself
to our home so he could get to know the family. Which — any
priest that's child orientated ... He was CYO, he had the altar boys
he was in charge of. That seems perfectly natural. He's around children all the time. So he came and he dropped down to meet the
family. And it just became he'd drop in when he wanted to drop in.
He'd talk to me about the prayer group, um, and things like that,
how he could be a help with the children. So he seemed like he was
a friend. Um. The way that I found out was that my sister made a
phone call to me and she had told me that my sons had been raped
by Father John Geoghan. And that I needed to speak to my sons.
And that's how I found out. And immediately after, I took the older
child and I separated him and I talked with him. And ... My child
became filled with fear. He was crying and shaking. He told me that
Father John Geoghan said that I wouldn't believe him. That I ...
had too much faith in the church ... and that I wouldn't believe

him. And then my son told me how things happened. He told me how Father Geoghan threatened him. And immediately my child tried to run out our back door — and I, I pulled my son back and I told my son that I would never, ever stop loving him. And I told my son that no way could Father Geoghan ever separate us. Well, the thing is, it separated us, it separated everybody in that ... I felt so guilty. I would dress my little four-year old and my little six-year and nine-year old and feed them, and thinking I was loving them so much and they would just look at you with the littlest, sweetest faces. And I caused their violation. If I hadn't invited that man into my house ... I'm the reason all of this has happened to everybody. I'm the guilty person. Um ... And I had to take care of it. And I did that. And I knew the vicar of this area and I went to that person. And he was overwhelmed. Because it was the first time he had ever heard of it. And he invited Father John Geoghan down to his house, to the rectory, had lunch with him. They sat across the table from each other, and when he asked Father John Geoghan — Father John Geoghan readily admitted it. And he said to the vicar, oh, well, it was only two families. *(Back to deposition. Krieger returns with McSorley. McSorley reseats himself.)*

KRIEGER.  Cardinal Law, are you familiar with what a mortal sin is?

CARDINAL.  Yes.

KRIEGER.  Could you briefly describe what a mortal sin is in lay-man's terms?

CARDINAL.  It's a strange kind of a question to have posed in a deposition in a civil suit, but I'm happy to try to —

KRIEGER.  Let me rephrase it. Is a mortal sin one that is incapable of absolution?

CARDINAL.  No.

KRIEGER.  It is capable of absolution?

CARDINAL.  Yes.

KRIEGER.  And are there any sins that are incapable of absolution?

CARDINAL.  Well, there's — scripture speaks of the unpardonable sin, and the unpardonable sin is the sin of thinking that there is the inability of receiving absolution. Absolution from sin necessitates certain things. First of all, it's the acknowledgement of the sin; it's sorrow for the sin; and it's a determination, insofar as is humanly possible and with the help of God's grace, to avoid that sin in the future. So it isn't — confession is not a revolving door.

KRIEGER.  Is raping a child an unpardonable sin if you are a priest?

VARLEY.  Objection. First amendment. This gets into the internal workings of the church.

KRIEGER. Is raping a child in any specific category of sin?

CARDINAL. That's a mortal sin.

KRIEGER. It's not an unpardonable sin?

CARDINAL. No. As I said, the unpardonable sin is a very specific term in scripture. Jesus came to save us from sin.

KRIEGER. Right.

CARDINAL. He died on the cross so — and took upon himself the burden of our sin. So that all of us, whatever our sin, if we are sorry for that sin, if we confess that sin, and if we seek to amend our life, are able to receive his pardon. And that's the meaning of his death on the cross.

KRIEGER. Now I would like to move on to Father Paul Shanley. Let's begin with Exhibit 37, a letter dated August 28, 1966, from a Father Arthur Chabot. *(Pronounced "Sha-bit." Spotlight on Father Chabot.)*

FATHER CHABOT. The parents of a boy in our parish came to me. They said Father Paul Shanley had molested the boy on a trip to a cabin in the Blue Hills. I believed them. I told them not to worry, that I had friends in the Chancery and that I would see that the matter would be taken care of. *(Back to deposition.)*

KRIEGER. You understand that this is a report of sexual abuse of a minor by Paul Shanley that was sent to the Archdiocese as far back as 1966?

CARDINAL. I wish I had been aware of this report. It is only possible to act based on what is known, however.

KRIEGER. So if you had been aware of this, you would have taken some action regarding Father Paul Shanley; correct?

CARDINAL. That's correct.

KRIEGER. And the action that you would have taken would have been the removal of —

CARDINAL. I would have —

KRIEGER. Excuse me. Let me finish the question. The action that you would have taken would have been the removal of Paul Shanley from ministry?

CARDINAL. Yes.

KRIEGER. Now let's talk about exhibit 38, letter from a Mrs. Dolores Stevens, dated October 4, 1977. *(Spotlight on Dolores Stevens.)*

DOLORES STEVENS. Regarding Father Paul Shanley, the following are some of his statements at a talk he gave at St. Luke's

Episcopalian Church in Rochester, New York. He spoke of pedophilia. He stated that the adult is not the seducer, that the "kid" is the seducer and further that the kid is not traumatized by the act per se, the kid is traumatized when the police and authorities "drag" the kid in for questioning. He stated that he can think of no sexual act that causes psychic damage. Father Shanley said he represented the Archdiocese of Boston and was wearing Roman collar. *(Back to deposition.)*

KRIEGER. Is this letter from Dolores Stevens the type of material that you wished you had in front of you in 1985 when you promoted Paul Shanley?

CARDINAL. Now, I have to tell you that my experience has been that in receiving these kinds of reports, Father so-and-so said such-and-such in his sermon, that one has to look into it carefully to be certain that what was said was said, that there wasn't a misunderstanding of what was said.

KRIEGER. But there would have been another report in the file, a letter marked exhibit 33, from attorney Paul McGeady, dated April 2, 1979. *(Spotlight of McGeady.)*

MCGEADY. Dear Bishop Daily. I thought you should be aware of an item from a publication called *Gaysweek* in which Father Shanley is designated as a representative of the archdiocese ... *(Clipping.)* "Father Paul Shanley told the story of a boy who was rejected by family and society, but helped by a boy-lover. When his parents found out about the relationship, however, the man was arrested, convicted and sent to prison. 'And there began the psychic demise of that kid,' Shanley commented. 'He had loved that man ... It was only a brief and passing thing as far as the sex was concerned, but the love was deep and the gratitude to the man was deep, and when he realized that the indiscretion in the eyes of society and the law had cost this man perhaps twenty years ... the boy began to fall apart?' Shanley concluded. 'We have our convictions upside down if we are truly concerned with boys ... the cure does far more damage.'" *(Back to deposition.)*

KRIEGER. That has a certain commonality with the report that was given by Dolores Stevens, does it not —

CARDINAL. Yes. Yes.

KRIEGER. Cardinal Law, would this letter have caused you to undertake some sort of inquiry concerning Paul Shanley and his suitability to serve as priest?

CARDINAL. Yes.

KRIEGER. So we have Bishop Daily, who would become your chief operating officer, directly involved in communications about Paul Shanley expressing his view on man-boy love; correct?

CARDINAL. Yes. Yes.

KRIEGER. There is another involvement of Bishop Daily. Turn to exhibit 28, a letter from Pastor Hugh Weston, dated May 4, 1983. *(Spotlight on Weston.)* Is it a fact that Father Paul Shanley represented you at the founding conference of NAMBLA, the North American Man-Boy Love Association? Please advise as to all details. *(Back to deposition.)*

KRIEGER. This was in your files, Cardinal Law.

CARDINAL. Excuse me. The Archdiocese's files. Not my files.

KRIEGER. Do you maintain separate files from the Archdiocese's files?

CARDINAL. No.

KRIEGER. At this time, you would have relied upon Bishop Daily to keep you updated on matters of importance; is that correct?

CARDINAL. That's correct.

KRIEGER. And that would include matters relating to priests; correct?

CARDINAL. That's correct.

KRIEGER. Bishop Daily was one of your closest advisors; correct?

CARDINAL. Yes.

KRIEGER. Would you consider him to be a friend?

CARDINAL. Oh, yes, I consider him a friend.

KRIEGER. Did Bishop Daily tell you anything about Paul Shanley making remarks about children having sex with adults, it's the fault of the child?

CARDINAL. No.

KRIEGER. You're certain of that?

CARDINAL. I am quite certain of that.

KRIEGER. Do you recall promoting Father Shanley in 1985 to pastor at St. Jean's?

CARDINAL. I've had that recalled to me.

KRIEGER. If you had known Paul Shanley's remarks about children having sex with adults, you would not have promoted him; correct?

VARLEY. Objection.

CARDINAL. My assumption is that Cardinal Medeiros would not have originally appointed Father Shanley associate pastor at St. Jean's if he hadn't been confident that he could do so with a clear conscience. As I've stated, when I arrived in Boston in 1984, I assumed that priests in place had been appointed appropriately.

KRIEGER. Bishop Daily had the Stevens letter, in which Paul Shanley was openly promoting or talking about sex with children; he had the McGeady letter, the Weston letter ... Do you believe Bishop Daily should have brought this to your attention before you promoted Paul Shanley to pastor in 1985?

VARLEY. I'm going to instruct the Cardinal not to answer the question. Since you are going to be deposing Bishop Daily on this, I want to get a ruling from the judge on this question.

KRIEGER. Well, what's —

VARLEY. Under these circumstances — I didn't mean to interrupt you.

KRIEGER. You can instruct your client not to answer, but it's — fine. *(To Cardinal.)* You're accepting your counsel's instructions not to answer my question about Bishop Daily?

CARDINAL. I'm going to accept counsel's instructions.

KRIEGER. Alright, then, Cardinal, let's look at a letter, number 63, that was not addressed to Bishop Daily, but directly to you. It's from a Wilma Higgs, dated April 29, 1985. *(Spotlight on Wilma Higgs.)*

WILMA HIGGS. Father Paul Shanley made some outlandish statements at a talk he gave here; some of his statements are on tape. He said: "When adults have sex with children, the children seduce them. Children may later regret having caused someone to go to prison, knowing that they are the guilty ones." The information he was giving was so blatantly untrue, I decided that it should be brought to attention of those in authority. *(Back to deposition.)*

CARDINAL. I do not recall having received this letter.

KRIEGER. Right.

CARDINAL. But this, again, is a report of what a priest said. What someone says he said.

KRIEGER. But you have the McGeady letter which attaches the article where Paul Shanley is reported as again stating his views about sex between adults and children. Does that not add a measure of credibility to Ms. Higgs's report?

CARDINAL. Certainly the compounding of evidence would do that.

KRIEGER. Ms. Higgs states she has a tape of some portion of the talk.

CARDINAL. She says — "Here are some of the statements; some

31

are on tape," — so I have no way of knowing which statement is on tape and which statement is her memory of what she heard.

KRIEGER. No inquiry was ever made to find out what was on the tape; is that correct, Cardinal?

CARDINAL. My presumption is that an appropriate inquiry concerning these allegations would have been made.

KRIEGER. "When adults have sex with children, the children seduce them. Children are the guilty ones." Would you agree with me that Father Shanley was making statements that were contrary to the teaching of the Roman Catholic Church?

CARDINAL. Clearly it would be contrary to the teaching of the Church. I think the issue here is whether or not he said that.

KRIEGER. We're going to get to that. Would this type of statement have caused you concern as to whether Father Shanley could remain in a parish with unsupervised access to children?

CARDINAL. Absolutely.

KRIEGER. So you would have expected those acting under your authority to investigate this allegation?

CARDINAL. Yes.

KRIEGER. You agree with me that this is a serious — I'm sorry. Mr. Varley, if we could just have — I see you're showing, for the record, the witness something that you've written down. If we could just have the Cardinal's testimony.

VARLEY. I don't think we've had anything but the Cardinal's testimony.

KRIEGER. I see you're writing something down and showing the Cardinal something.

VARLEY. I've been noting things before and you made no comment on it.

KRIEGER. Cardinal Law, do you know what happened after the letter from Ms. Higgs was received at the Archdiocese?

CARDINAL. I do not know.

KRIEGER. There was a response. From your delegate, Father John McCormack. Please turn to exhibit 129, May 15, 1985. *(Spot on McCormack.)*

BISHOP MCCORMACK. Dear Ms. Higgs. Archbishop Law received your letter. He is sorry to hear you were disturbed about the talk given by Father Paul Shanley and asked that I respond on his behalf. *(Back to deposition.)*

KRIEGER. This seems to reference a discussion that Father McCormack had with you about the Higgs letter.

VARLEY. I object. Is that a question?

KRIEGER. This is a letter from your files by Father McCormack which states that you received Ms. Higgs's letter. It states: "He" — meaning you — "is sorry to hear that you were disturbed about the talk and asked that I respond on his behalf." Would you agree that a fair reading of that sentence is that you and Father McCormack had some discussion about the Higgs letter?

CARDINAL. I would agree that that is a possible reading, but another meaning is that Father McCormack is acting in my name.

KRIEGER. Well, what we do know is that Father McCormack wrote to Wilma Higgs and expressed your sentiments —

CARDINAL. Which he would have —

KRIEGER. Excuse me. Let me just finish. — expressed your sentiments about the letter received from Ms. Higgs, correct?

CARDINAL. Father McCormack adequately reflected here what he knew my sentiments would be in this kind of a situation, yes.

KRIEGER. Well, he didn't say that he knew what your sentiments would be; he stated what they were.

CARDINAL. I understand what the letter says.

KRIEGER. That would have to involve some communication between you necessarily and Father McCormack on the subject of the Higgs letter; correct?

CARDINAL. Not necessarily.

KRIEGER. I'd like you to turn to 944, a letter from Father McCormack to Paul Shanley, dated June 4, 1985. *(Spotlight on McCormack.)*

BISHOP MCCORMACK. Recently I received a note from the Cardinal about a letter he had received from Wilma Higgs. It pertained to a talk you gave in the Rochester area last November. *(Back to deposition.)*

KRIEGER. So at this time, back some seventeen years ago, Father McCormack is reporting that he had received some note from you about the Higgs letter; correct?

CARDINAL. That's correct.

KRIEGER. Would it be a fair reading that there was at one point a note that you had sent to Father McCormack about the Higgs letter?

CARDINAL. And the note could have said: "Please follow up on this, look into this."

KRIEGER. But this letter suggests it was more than that — that, in fact, you did read the letter from Ms. Higgs and wrote Father McCormack, which prompted him to bring this to the attention of

Father Shanley. Is that a fair statement?

CARDINAL. I would presume that that's a reasonable assumption.

KRIEGER. So can we agree that it's more probable than not that you did, in fact, read the Higgs letter?

CARDINAL. Yes.

KRIEGER. Please turn to 813, a sworn affidavit from Ms. Jackie Gauvreau. *(Spotlight on Gauvreau.)*

GAUVREAU. In 1985, I confronted Cardinal Law about the allegation against Father Shanley. On the day I confronted him, I had sung in a choir in a televised mass he conducted. After the mass, I told him face-to-face that Father Shanley had molested a child while he was a priest at St. Jean's. In response, Cardinal Law told me he would look into the matter. Father Shanley, however, remained a priest at St. Jean's and I do not know of any actions were taken against him. *(Back to deposition.)*

CARDINAL. I have absolutely no recollection of that conversation having taken place.

KRIEGER. Do you have a recollection of this conversation with Ms. Gauvreau, Cardinal Law? *(Spotlight on Gauvreau.)*

GAUVREAU. Sometime soon after, I had a second opportunity to speak to Cardinal Law about the matter. While Cardinal Law was present at Our Lady Help in Newton, I asked him what he intended to do about Father Shanley. In response, he told me to contact the bishop, stating "That is why I have my bishops." So I visited the bishop for my parish, Bishop Mulcahy, just like Cardinal Law asked me to. Bishop Mulcahy listened to my complaints about Father Shanley sexually molesting children. I do not know what action, if any, he took to investigate the allegation other than ask Father Shanley to apologize — to me! *(Back to deposition.)*

KRIEGER. Are you still comfortable with your response of having no recollection of any meeting with Ms. Gauvreau? *(Varley whispers to Cardinal.)* I would just ask that, respectfully, that we not speak with counsel during the questions.

CARDINAL. I don't believe I have initiated any conversation.

KRIEGER. The record will show that Mr. Varley had conversations with the Cardinal where there's been a question pending.

VARLEY. We can carry on this nonsensical conversation as much as you like because it appears you're running out of questions.

KRIEGER. So you won't talk to the Cardinal?

VARLEY. Do you have a question to ask or shall we leave?

KRIEGER. You can leave if you want to.

VARLEY. No, no.

KRIEGER. Are you still comfortable with your response of having no recollection of any meeting with Ms. Gauvreau?

CARDINAL. Yes, I am.

KRIEGER. Cardinal Law, let's look at 217, a letter dated July 10, 1986, from an individual who works for the Massachusetts Department of Social Services. It's on official letterhead — "Commonwealth of Massachusetts, Executive Office of Human Services, Department of Social Services." This is a letter from an employee of a government agency; correct?

CARDINAL. Yes.

KRIEGER. The letter starts by referencing a TV program where the topic of sexual abuse of children by parish priests came up ... *(Spot on DSS Employee.)*

DSS EMPLOYEE. The TV special talked about how the Catholic Church did not acknowledge the problem, enforce sanctions on priests who were involved in such cases and simply transferred the priest to another unsuspecting parish. *(Back to deposition.)*

KRIEGER. So here we have a letter which expresses concern about the transfer of priests to unsuspecting parishes after there's been an allegation of abuse; is that correct?

CARDINAL. Well, this is a letter which speaks about a television show that makes that allegation.

KRIEGER. Right.

CARDINAL. I must say that this is a letter that I do not recall ever having seen.

KRIEGER. But you understand, Cardinal Law, that this is a letter from a government agency?

CARDINAL. I see on the letterhead. *(Spotlight on DSS Employee.)*

DSS EMPLOYEE. As a former victim of sexual misuse by a number of diocesan priests, I have witnessed firsthand the pain and anguish that such an incident can incur. *(Back to deposition.)*

KRIEGER. Is it not a fair reading of this letter that this man is reporting that he has been victimized by diocesan priests?

CARDINAL. It certainly appears to be the case.

KRIEGER. And it's plural; not just one?

CARDINAL. Yes. *(Spotlight on DSS Employee.)*

DSS EMPLOYEE. If you are interested in hearing more about the circumstances of my past experiences as a victim and its continuing emotional effects, perhaps we can schedule a meeting. *(Back to deposition.)*

KRIEGER. Here is a state official charged with protecting children telling you that he has been victimized by a number of diocesan priests — and asking "if you're interested in hearing more about this, we can schedule a meeting."

VARLEY. Is that a question?

KRIEGER. Yes, it is.

VARLEY. It's argumentative and inappropriate.

KRIEGER. Cardinal, he's willing to talk to you about his experience as a victim. Is that what his letter says?

CARDINAL. Anyone coming forward in this way would have been met with for the sake of determining if children were at risk.

KRIEGER. Then let's turn to 986, your secretary, Father Helmick's response, dated August 19, 1986. Would you please read it?

CARDINAL. "His Eminence, Cardinal Law, has asked me to respond to your letter of July 10. You may be sure that — "

KRIEGER. That seems to suggest that you had a conversation with Father Helmick about this letter; does it not?

CARDINAL. There can also be an implicit understanding that there are matters the secretary may respond to in my name without my having discussed the matter with him; that's part of his job.

KRIEGER. Do you know that your secretary was deposed in this very room two days ago?

CARDINAL. No.

KRIEGER. He testified under oath that he would have spoken to you about this letter because he was not authorized to state that he had spoken to you or met with you about a particular piece of correspondence unless he actually had done that. In light of all that, Cardinal Law, can you state unequivocally that you did not see it?

VARLEY. I believe he already stated — asked and answered.

KRIEGER. Please read the rest of Father Helmick's letter, Cardinal Law, if you would.

CARDINAL. "You may be sure that any incident of sexual abuse of a child by anyone is viewed most seriously by the church. If there were to be an incident of such abuse by a priest, you can be sure that the matter would be taken most seriously with deep concern for the victim, the people and the priest."

KRIEGER. Father Helmick's response did not follow-up on his offer to meet, to discuss his experiences, correct?

CARDINAL. That's correct.

KRIEGER. And was that consistent with your policy concerning allegations of sexual misconduct by priests?

CARDINAL. Let me say, Mr. Krieger, even though this person uses, you know, rather — not very forceful about the idea of a meeting.

KRIEGER. But Father Helmick's letter doesn't address that, does it?

CARDINAL. Father Helmick's letter does not address that.

KRIEGER. If there had been such a meeting, would you be surprised to learn that this gentleman would have reported to you allegations concerning Father Paul Shanley?

CARDINAL. The letter doesn't mention anyone.

KRIEGER. After Father Helmick responded to the letter, the person at the Department of Social Services sent back another letter, only this one was addressed to you. This is exhibit 73. *(Spot on DSS Employee.)*

DSS EMPLOYEE. Dear Cardinal Law. I have received the letter which you asked Father Helmick to write me. I must state my deep concern regarding this response. *(Reads from the letter.)* "If there were to be an incident of abuse by a priest, you can be sure that the matter would be taken most seriously." Very appropriate and responsible on the surface. Unfortunately, this response negates the fact that I am aware of such incidents from my own experience as a victim. I can't help but wonder on what basis Father Helmick is questioning my experience as a victim. By not believing an honest and revealing statement by a victim, you are altering your own perception of reality. In doing so, it becomes much easier to believe you are responding appropriately. I implore you to step forward into a perception of reality and come to understand and believe that such incidents do occur. By adopting this frame of reference, you can honestly answer whether or not you are answering appropriately. *(Back to deposition.)*

KRIEGER. Do you remember receiving that letter, Cardinal Law?

CARDINAL. I do not.

KRIEGER. Moving forward, to 1989, please turn to a memo, 41, written by your delegate, Father McCormack. *(Spotlight on McCormack.)*

BISHOP MCCORMACK. Father Shanley is so personally damaged that his pathology is beyond repair. It cannot be reversed. How do we protect others from him? *(Back to deposition.)*

CARDINAL. I don't have a recollection of this being communicated to me, but it might well have been.

KRIEGER. In 1989, you asked for Paul Shanley's resignation from his parish assignment, correct?

CARDINAL. I'm not sure that I asked for his resignation. He did have health problems. I suggested that maybe the best thing for him to do was just deal with those health problems.

KRIEGER. Out in California?

CARDINAL. Well, I didn't say California. It was his desire to go to California.

KRIEGER. Please turn to 42, a letter dated January 16, 1990, drafted by your delegate, Bishop Robert Banks, to Reverend Behan at the diocese of San Bernardino in California. *(Spotlight on Bishop Banks.)*

BISHOP BANKS. Reverend Paul Shanley, a priest in good standing and of the Archdiocese of Boston, was recently granted a medical leave for one year by His Eminence Cardinal Law. He plans to live in the area of Palm Springs, California, during this time. Afterwards he plans to return to the Archdiocese of Boston for an assignment. His Eminence, Cardinal Law, will appreciate whatever assistance can be given to Father Shanley. I can assure you that Father Shanley has no problems that would be a concern to your diocese. He has resigned from his parish on his own; we shall place him in parish ministry when he returns. With warm regards, I am sincerely yours in Christ. *(Back to deposition.)*

KRIEGER. Are you aware that there are allegations of sexual abuse against minors by Father Shanley out in California?

CARDINAL. I have heard that, yes.

KRIEGER. And you've apologized personally, have you not, to the Bishop of San Bernadino?

CARDINAL. I certainly have.

KRIEGER. Please turn to a memo written by Father McCormack dated December 9, 1991, exhibit 52. *(Spotlight on Father McCormack.)*

BISHOP MCCORMACK. It is clear that Paul Shanley is a sick person. I really question the advisability of asking him to return from California for psychiatric consultation with the view that he would be able to return to active ministry in Boston. *(Back to deposition.)*

KRIEGER. Have you ever seen language like that about any priest of the Archdiocese of Boston, Cardinal Law?

VARLEY. Objection.

KRIEGER. At least by December of 1991, your delegate is questioning whether Shanley should be returned to Boston. Do you see that?

CARDINAL. Yes.

KRIEGER. In fact, Father Shanley didn't come back to Boston, he went to New York City; correct?

CARDINAL. Yes.

KRIEGER. And that he was working at a place called Leo House on West Twenty-third Street in New York City?

CARDINAL. Yes.

KRIEGER. And you understood that that was a hotel for Catholic travelers and other individuals?

CARDINAL. I was not aware that it was a place where families could lodge, where children could lodge.

KRIEGER. Turn to 128, a memo to you from Father Flatley, dated September 13, 1995. *(Spot on Father Flatley.)*

FATHER FLATLEY. Father Shanley has been working at Leo House since February of 1995. One of his accusers keeps a close watch on him, and he called here, upset that Father Shanley is working in a place where children reside. *(Back to deposition.)*

KRIEGER. So given the fact that you would have read Father Flatley's memo, would you like to modify your earlier testimony that you thought that Leo House was a place where only priests resided?

CARDINAL. I received this memo and I presume it must have registered with me.

KRIEGER. But you took no action to remove Paul Shanley; correct?

CARDINAL. I did not take an action to remove him.

KRIEGER. This is a letter, exhibit 103, dated December 14, 1995, from Sister Anne Karlin who worked at Leo House. *(Spot on Sister Anne.)*

SR ANNE. Last evening, I received a phone call from the Boston area, presumably from a priest. I am somewhat disturbed because after throwing out some wild accusations, he openly said that Father Paul Shanley was a child molester and we had better beware! I didn't think that this person had any justification to state all that he did, but he ended up saying he would have to make it known to the New York *Times*! I'm sitting on a time bomb here. Would you be so kind as to clarify Father Paul's integrity and reputation and character. *(Back to deposition.)*

KRIEGER. This letter was addressed to you — and it was produced from your files. Do you see that?

CARDINAL. I see that.

KRIEGER. It does not contain the stamp *Not Acknowledged at Cardinal's Residence.*

CARDINAL. That's correct.

KRIEGER. Do you have a recollection of receiving it?

CARDINAL. I do not.

KRIEGER. In 1995, Cardinal, you were informed that Paul Shanley had been offered the job of director of Leo House; is that correct?

CARDINAL. That's correct.

KRIEGER. You were asked to give your permission for this promotion to go through; correct?

CARDINAL. Yes.

KRIEGER. And you were willing to go along, were you not?

CARDINAL. I was willing to approach the Archbishop of New York about this possibility.

KRIEGER. Cardinal O'Connor, that would be, correct?

CARDINAL. That's correct. And a letter was prepared for my signature, which never went, because in the intervening time, it was clear that Cardinal O'Connor was not open to this idea, and that was good for me, and so I never sent the letter.

KRIEGER. Well, you were prepared to go along with Paul Shanley's promotion if Cardinal O'Connor had no objection, correct?

CARDINAL. I have to say I was not pleased with this possibility, but, yes, I would have sent that letter with my approval.

KRIEGER. Even though you were aware that Leo House was a place where children resided; correct?

CARDINAL. I had the knowledge that medically Father Shanley's own situation had changed in terms of sexual activity.

KRIEGER. You believe that because there was a — some problem with his prostate, that Paul Shanley would no longer be a threat to children — is that your testimony?

CARDINAL. I had the impression from some of that information that he would not be a threat sexually; that he would not be a — that he would not be acting out sexually. That was my understanding.

KRIEGER. Did an expert tell you that or a medical doctor?

CARDINAL. Well, I believe that that's based on a medical — certainly I wouldn't have had the ability to make that kind of a judgment.

KRIEGER. Was it your understanding in 1997 that individuals who act out sexually against children are doing so because of some sexual urge that would be ameliorated by a deterioration of their prostate?

CARDINAL. You know, generally, I was under the impression that the psychosexual urge was sometime — somehow connected to — the physiognomy and the psychology were linked. I may be wrong on that.

KRIEGER. I'd like us to look at a letter you wrote to Paul Shanley, dated February 29, 1996, exhibit 141, after he was informed that he would not get to be director of Leo House. Would you please read it?

CARDINAL. "Dear Father Shanley. This letter provides me with an opportunity to thank you in my name and in the name of the people of the Archdiocese for the ministry which you offered, both in parishes and in a specialized way over the years from your ordination in 1960 until your sick leave began in 1990. For thirty years in assigned ministry, you brought God's word and his love to his people. That is an impressive record and all of us are truly grateful for your priestly care and ministry to all whom you have served during those years. Without doubt, the lives and hearts of many people have been touched by your sharing of the Lord's spirit. You are truly appreciated for all that you have done. With grateful remembrance and with my blessing and promise of prayer, I remain, Sincerely yours in Christ."

KRIEGER. Those were your words to Paul Shanley?

CARDINAL. That's correct. These are my words to a priest who, in the course of his many years of active ministry, did, in effect, preach God's word, share God's love to a number of people in an effective way.

KRIEGER. And committed unspeakable evil?

CARDINAL. And committed unspeakable evil, that's correct. And one of the reasons … It's a question of trying to be pastoral and reconciling to somebody who still remains a human being even though he has done terrible, terrible things.

KRIEGER. What, Cardinal Law, were you specifically doing to reach out and help the victims of Paul Shanley's unspeakable evil?

CARDINAL. This letter is an attempt to deal with the perpetrator. With regard to outreach to victims, again, that was the responsibility of the Delegate.

KRIEGER. My question is in terms of what you personally did for the victims of this unspeakable evil. *(No response from the Cardinal.)* Have you concluded with your answer?

CARDINAL. I have.

KRIEGER. Do you remember assigning Father Paul Mahan to St. Matthews?

CARDINAL. Yes.

KRIEGER. Were you aware there were allegations of sexual misconduct against him?

CARDINAL. I was not.

KRIEGER. Do you know a Father Jack Connoll?

41

CARDINAL. I do.

KRIEGER. Has he been accused of sexual misconduct?

CARDINAL. He has.

KRIEGER. Do you know Father Jon Martin?

CARDINAL. I do.

KRIEGER. And you're aware there is an allegation against him of sexual misconduct with a minor?

CARDINAL. I cannot speak with any specificity about the allegation.

KRIEGER. Are you generally aware that there was an allegation of sexual misconduct made against Father Martin?

CARDINAL. I could not give you any kind of specifics. I just don't know.

KRIEGER. I'm not asking about any specifics. Maybe I'm misreading your answer or I'm not doing the question properly. Are you generally aware that there's been an allegation of sexual misconduct brought against Father Jon Martin?

CARDINAL. I know he was sent for treatment. But I can't recall the specifics.

KRIEGER. Do you know Father Gale?

CARDINAL. I do, yes.

KRIEGER. And you know that there have been allegations of sexual attacks against minors about Father Gale?

CARDINAL. All right.

KRIEGER. Do you know Father Graham?

CARDINAL. Yes.

KRIEGER. You're aware of allegations against Father Graham, is that correct?

CARDINAL. Allegations, yes.

KRIEGER. Do you know Father Rosenkranz?

CARDINAL. Yes.

KRIEGER. You're aware of allegations against him, is that correct?

CARDINAL. Yes.

KRIEGER. Do you know Father John Picardi?

CARDINAL. I do.

KRIEGER. Do you recall, Cardinal, that Father Picardi was accused of sexual misconduct in a schoolyard with a girl?

CARDINAL. Yes.

KRIEGER. Do you know Father Rebeiro?

CARDINAL. I do.

KRIEGER. Are you aware of allegations against Father Rebeiro?

CARDINAL. Yes.

KRIEGER. In each one of these cases, after there was an allegation of sexual molestation, in each one of those incidents, the priest was returned to active ministry in a parish; is that correct?

CARDINAL. I believe that's correct, yes.

KRIEGER. And that even includes Father O'Sullivan who had been convicted in a criminal prosecution regarding sexual abuse; correct?

CARDINAL. That's correct.

KRIEGER. Can you identify one priest who had allegations of sexual molestation against him who was removed from parish ministry at this time — one priest?

CARDINAL. I don't believe that there are any.

KRIEGER. Did you ever think that there was some need for action, even if it just involved getting the priests together and saying: This is intolerable. This type of conduct is intolerable. Do you understand my question?

CARDINAL. I understand the answer that you want me to give.

KRIEGER. Okay, Cardinal Law. I have no further questions.

*(Cardinal Law and Varley gather their things and exit. Patrick McSorley stands as Law passes by on his way out.)*

SPEAKER #1. In 2002, Cardinal Bernard Law resigned as Archbishop of Boston. He remains a Cardinal. In 2004, Pope John Paul II appointed him Archpriest of Santa Maria Maggiore basilica in Rome, where he now resides.

SPEAKER #2. The Attorney General of Massachusetts estimates the number of children abused in the Archdiocese of Boston over the past six decades likely exceeds one thousand.

PATRICK MCSORLEY. My father committed suicide when I was six years old. The reason Father Geoghan had come to my mother's house was to give us his condolences — see, now, this was six years after my father's death ... And he, uh, asked my mother if he could take me out for an ice cream. And you know, he was a priest. And to me — I grew up in a, you know, a lower-class, you know, poor, you could say, neighborhood. And, um, I didn't, I didn't know Father Geoghan and at first it was, it seemed a little strange to me that a priest would just come by out of the blue that I didn't know, but he offered to take me out for an ice cream and I jumped at the chance because I was a poor kid and an ice cream was kind of a big deal. On the way back, um, while we were in the car he, uh — this is really what gets me right here — it, it, you know, it still hurts and I get very angry when I think about it … Um. You know … I had shorts on, it was the summertime. And, uh, he asked, you know, you know, how's everything, how you doin' — in the middle of all that he started to tell me that he was sorry about my father's death, started to pat me on the leg. You know — sorry to hear about your father's death. Before I knew it his hands were up my shorts and he was grabbing at me. From what I could see, he had, there was something … He was going back and forth from the wheel to himself. And he had grabbed … I remember … I remember him grabbing napkins — and he gave one to me and kept the rest for himself. That's very sick. Uh, he, uh … We were driving on Brush Hill Road — he took the long way back. He, uh — I just remember him goin' real slow, goin' back and forth from the wheel to himself. And, uh …

KRIEGER. Patrick McSorley died of a drug overdose a year after the conclusion of these proceedings. He was twenty-nine.

PATRICK MCSORLEY. Uh, I just remember — I was shocked, petrified. I couldn't talk. I couldn't move. My stomach was playing tricks on me. There was nothing I could do about it. You know, he must have sensed that I was very uncomfortable with what he was doing, 'cause he, you know, he ended up slowly taking his hand out and getting me back to my house. But I just remember him getting out of the car and him asking me if I wanted him to make a return visit — and I was standing there on the sidewalk in front of my house with the ice cream all melted, all melted down my arm, and I just remember him smilin' at me as his car was driving off. Before he took off, I remember him saying, Let's just — just you and me. No one else has to know about this.

**End of Play**

# PROPERTY LIST

Flag stand
American flag
Water dispenser
5-gallon water bottle
Water cups
Lateral filing cabinet
Vertical storage cabinet
Conference room table
Conference table chairs
Coffee maker
Coffee cups
Sugar
Creamer
Stirrers
Dead plant
Computer desk
Credenza
Trash can
Various legal books
Various papers
File boxes with evidence letters
Luggage dolly
2 letters in red report covers
2 pens
2 three-ring binders with evidence letters
2 legal pads
2 microphones on table
Mic stands
Telephone
*Gaysweek* magazine clipping
2 briefcases
Coffee cup
Crucifix
Cardinal's ring
Eye glasses
Handkerchief
Bible
Stool
Higg's letter from Bishop McCormack

Letters
Awards
Desk set
Book ends
Rolodex
Telephone books
File boxes
Computer monitor
Adding machine
Stapler
Scotch tape
Letter opener
Paper clip holder
Electric typewriter
Banker's lamp
Paper towels
Tissue boxes
Coffee filters